A Letter to our Daughters

Jodi L. Leffingwell Ed.D

This book is dedicated to my daughters Abigale and Aubrey. It is dedicated to mothers, daughters, and women everywhere who need a reminder that they are a gift to this world.

To my mother, who truly made me believe that I could do anything.

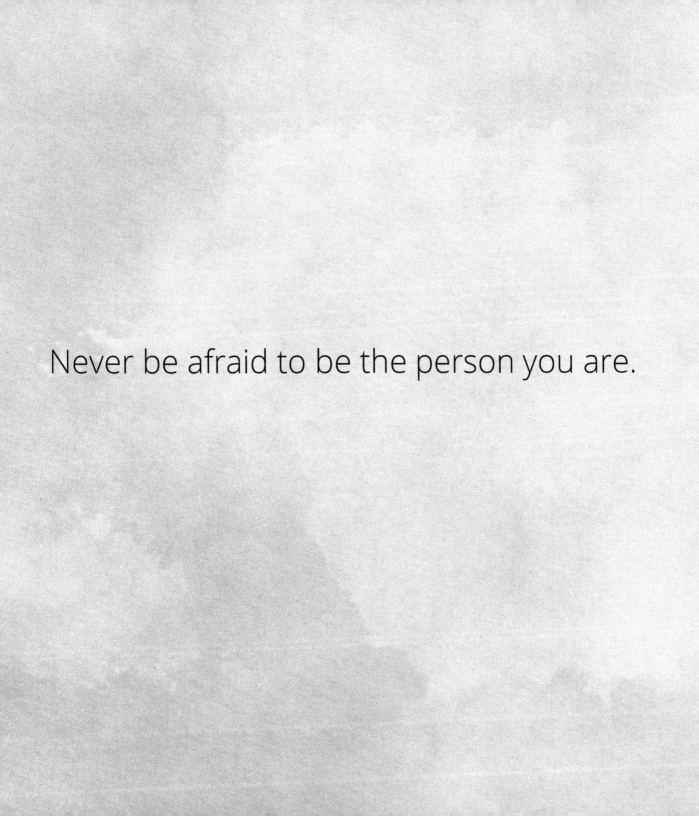

Never be afraid to be the person you are.

Never be afraid to fail. It is where all the learning happens.

Never be the smartest
person in the room.

If you are, then you are in the wrong room

Always walk into a room
like you own it.

Head up!

Shoulders back!

Forgive yourself for making mistakes.

You will make a million.

Never be afraid to tell your mother anything.

Mama's wear bulletproof vests.

Be kind!

Be independent!

Be happy!

Don't apologize for being happy!

The world will demand it.

Do the things that scare you!

Love with your whole heart.

You will be hurt and that's ok.

It is what helps you grow.

Be true to yourself, regardless
of what people say.

Never feel the need to be popular.
Popularity is fleeting
and highly overrated.

Assert yourself.

Never let anyone tell you that you cannot achieve your goals.

Work hard!

Stay humble!

It may not always turn out as you want,
but it will turn out for the best.

You can be smart and beautiful.

Never apologize for being both.

You are talented.

You have gifts to offer the world.

Use them to help others.

Be fierce and comfortable in your own skin.

People will disappoint you and many times it will not have anything to do with you at all.

Know that there will always be someone there to

Lift you up,

Cheer you on,

And guide you.

Stay classy.

Stay sassy.

And even a little bad-assy!

YOU

ARE A

GIFT TO THIS WORLD.

IT IS YOUR TIME TO SHINE!

CPSIA information can be obtained
at www.ICGtesting.com
Printed in the USA
BVHW010820280222
629770BV00038B/473

9 781387 081400